Exploring
North America

Continents of the World
Geography Series

By
MICHAEL KRAMME, PH.D.

COPYRIGHT 2003 Mark Twain Media, Inc.

ISBN 1-58037-223-6

Printing No. CD-1569

Mark Twain Media, Inc., Publishers
Distributed by Carson-Dellosa Publishing Company, Inc.

Map Source: Mountain High Maps® Copyright © 1993 Digital Wisdom, Inc.

Table of Contents

The Continents

A continent is a large land-mass completely or mostly surrounded by water. Geographers list seven continents: North America, South America, Europe, Asia, Africa, Australia, and Antarctica. Greenland and the India-Pakistan area are sometimes referred to as "subcontinents." Madagascar and the Seychelles Islands are often called "microcontinents." The island groups in the Pacific Ocean are called "Oceania," but they are not considered a continent.

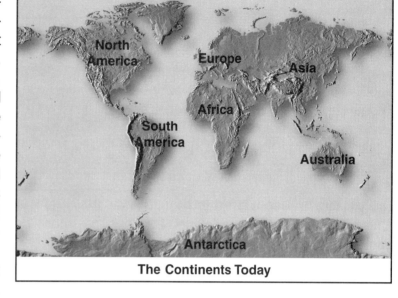

The Continents Today

The continents make up just over 29 percent of the earth's surface. They occupy about 57,100,000 square miles (148,000,000 sq. km). More than 65 percent of the land area is in the Northern Hemisphere.

HOW WERE THE CONTINENTS FORMED?

For many years, Europeans believed the continents were formed by a catastrophe or series of catastrophes, such as floods, earthquakes, and volcanoes. In 1596, a Dutch mapmaker, Abraham Ortelius, noted that the Americas' eastern coasts and the western coasts of Europe and Africa looked as if they fit together. He proposed that once they had been joined but later were torn apart.

Many years later, a German named Alfred Lothar Wegener published a book in which he explained his theory of the "**Continental Drift**." Wegener, like Ortelius, believed that the earth originally had one super continent. He named it **Pangaea** from the Greek word meaning "all lands." He believed that the large landmass was a lighter rock that floated on a heavier rock, like ice floats on water.

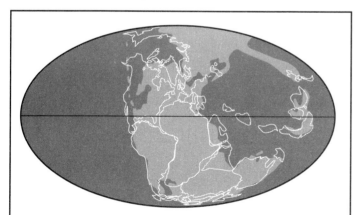

Wegener's theoretical continent, Pangaea, during the Permian Age (white outlines indicate current continents)

Wegener's theory stated that the landmasses were still moving at a rate of about one yard each century. Wegener believed that Pangaea existed in the Permian Age. Then Pangaea slowly divided into two continents, the upper part, **Laurasia**, and the lower, **Gondwanaland**, during the Triassic Age.

1

By the Jurassic Age, the land-masses had moved into what we could recognize as the seven continents, although they were still located near each other. Eventually, the continents "drifted" to their present locations.

Most scientists had been in agreement on the continental drift theory until researchers in the 1960s discovered several major mountain ranges on the ocean floor. These mountains suggested that the earth's crust consists of about 20 slabs or **plates**.

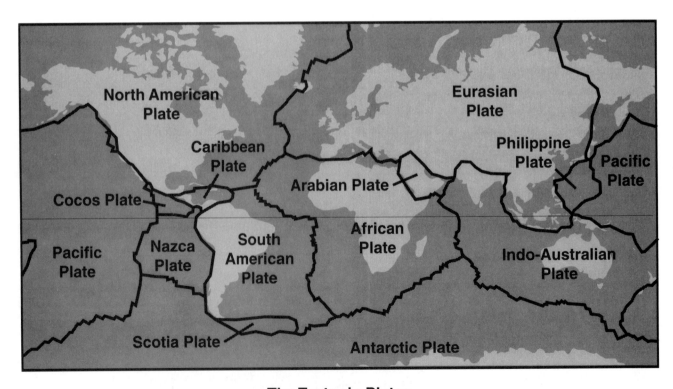

Landmasses during the Jurassic Age

These discoveries led to a new theory, "**Plate Tectonics**," which has become more popular. This theory suggests that these plates move a few inches each year. In some places the plates are moving apart, while in others, the plates are colliding or scraping against each other.

Scientists also discovered that most volcanoes and earthquakes occur along the boundaries of the various plates. They hope that further study will help them increase their understanding of Earth's story.

The Tectonic Plates

Name: _____ Date: _____

Questions for Consideration

1. What is a continent? _____

   _____

2. The continents make up what percentage of the earth's surface?

   _____

3. What was the name of Wegener's theory?

   _____

4. What is the name of the newer theory that replaced Wegener's?

   _____

5. What two natural happenings occur near the boundaries of the plates?

   _____

Map Project

On the map below, label all seven of the continents.

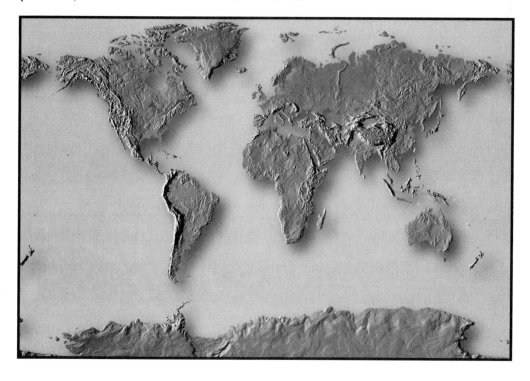

Name: _____ Date: _____

Outline Map of North America

The Continent of North America

North America is the third largest of the seven continents. It includes Canada, the United States, Mexico, Greenland, the countries of Central America, and the West Indies islands.

North America covers over 9,200,000 square miles (23,800,000 sq. km). Together with South America, North America forms the land in what is known as the Western Hemisphere.

North America is bordered on the east by the Atlantic Ocean, on the west by the Pacific Ocean, on the north by the Arctic Ocean and on the south by the Gulf of Mexico. It is separated from South America

by the border between Panama and Colombia. Some geographers claim that the Isthmus of Panama actually divides the two continents.

The continent's lowest point is Death Valley, California. It is 282 feet (86 m) below sea level. The highest point is Mount McKinley in Alaska. It is 20,320 feet (6,194 m) above sea level.

The continent has five major regions. The Canadian Shield includes eastern Canada, most of Greenland, and part of the northern United States. Part of the region is frozen wasteland, and other parts contain poor soil and large forests.

A coastal plain covers most of the eastern United States and Mexico. The third region is a narrow strip that contains many hills and the Appalachian Mountains of the United States.

The fourth region includes the central plain extending from southern Canada to Texas. This region includes most of the continent's agricultural lands. It is mainly flat land, but has some hilly regions.

The fifth region is the western part of the continent and includes the western United States and Canada and most of Mexico. This region includes the Rocky Mountains of the United States and Canada and the Sierra Madres of southern California and Mexico.

Major river systems include the Great Lakes and St. Lawrence River, which drain into

the northern Atlantic Ocean. The Mississippi and Missouri Rivers drain most of the central United States and part of southern Canada into the Gulf of Mexico. The Mackenzie River, which flows into the Hudson Bay, drains much of western Canada.

Most of North America's lakes are in the northern part of the continent. Lake Superior is the world's largest freshwater lake. Other major lakes include the remainder of the Great Lakes: Erie, Huron, Michigan, and Ontario, as well as Lake Mead on the Colorado River, and the Great Salt Lake in Utah.

Name: _____ Date: _____

Questions for Consideration

1. Together, what do North America and South America form?

   _____

2. What is North America's lowest point?

   _____

3. What is North America's highest point?

   _____

4. What major river drains into Hudson Bay?

   _____

5. Name the five "Great Lakes." _____

   _____

Map Project

Using an atlas or globe and the outline map of North America (located on page 4), label the following:

Bodies of Water:

Arctic Ocean

Atlantic Ocean

Gulf of Mexico

Pacific Ocean

The Great Lakes

The Mississippi River

Hudson Bay

Land Features:

Appalachian Mountains

Rocky Mountains

Sierra Madres

DID YOU KNOW?

North America covers just over 16 percent of the world's surface, yet has only five percent of the world's population.

North America's Climate

North America has the full range of climate types, ranging from arctic in the far north to tropical in the south.

Alaska, Greenland, and northern Canada have **arctic** and **subarctic** climates. The region is covered with snow and ice during all or most of the year. The winters are bitterly cold with long nights and short days. The southern part of this region has short, mild summers, while the northern part includes vast amounts of tundra.

Humid continental climate regions of North America include some of southern Canada and the northeast fourth of the United States. The humid continental climate includes cold winters and hot summers, with adequate amounts of precipitation.

The southeastern part of the United States is in a **humid subtropical** climate zone. Here, the winters are often warm, and the summers are hot and humid.

☐	Ice Cap
■	Tundra
▨	Subarctic
▨	Desert
▨	Tropical Savanna
■	Tropical Rain Forest
▤	Humid Continental, Cool Summer
▨	Undifferentiated Highlands
☐	Humid Continental, Warm Summer
■	Mediterranean
▨	Marine West Coast

North American climate map

The northwestern part of the United States and the southwest corner of Canada have a **highland** climate. This region has mild winters and warm summers. It also has significant amounts of precipitation.

Most of the western United States experiences **semidesert** and **desert** climates. These regions have hot daytime temperatures with cool nights and very little rainfall.

The west coast of the United States includes both **marine west coast** and **Mediterranean** climates. These regions have moderate temperatures and adequate rainfall.

Mexico's climate zones include **desert** and **semidesert** regions as well as some **highland** and **tropical** areas. Rainfall amounts in these regions vary, but the winters are usually mild, and the summers are hot.

Parts of southern Mexico and most of Central America are in a **tropical** climate zone. This climate features hot temperatures and much rainfall throughout the year. Tropical rain forests are common in the Central American countries.

The western United States and parts of Mexico include desert regions.

Name: _____ Date: _____

Questions for Consideration

1. What are the two extremes of climates in North America?

   _____

2. What best describes the seasons in a humid continental climate?

   _____

3. What is the climate of the southeastern part of the United States?

   _____

4. What two climates does the western coast of the United States have?

   _____

5. In what part of North America are rain forests common?

   _____

DID YOU KNOW?

Over four-fifths of Greenland is covered by a layer of ice. The ice has an average depth of about 5,000 feet (1,500 m).

Climate Zones

Describe the main features of the following climates:

1. Arctic: _____

   _____

2. Humid continental: _____

   _____

3. Humid subtropical: _____

   _____

4. Highland: _____

   _____

5. Desert: _____

   _____

6. Tropical: _____

   _____

Fish can be caught even in the winter by drilling holes in the ice.

North America's Resources and Industries

North America has a wide variety of industries and valuable natural resources.

Large deposits of petroleum and natural gas are in Alaska, western Canada, the southwestern United States, and eastern Mexico. Proposals for new drilling in Alaska have continued to bring protests from environmentalists. Even with its large deposits, the United States imports a large amount of petroleum each year.

Coal is mined in large quantities in the United States and Canada. Great amounts of iron ore come from the United States, Canada, and Mexico.

Other plentiful minerals include copper, lead, nickel, sulfur, uranium, and zinc. Gold and silver are also mined throughout the continent.

North America has a wide range of industries. Both Canada and the United States are highly industrialized. Mexico and the Central American countries are less developed, but they are becoming more industrialized. Major industries include electronics, food and beverage processing, chemicals, forest and paper products, machinery, motor vehicles, clothing, and textiles.

Agriculture is a major industry throughout much of the continent. It is highly mechanized in Canada and the United States. In Mexico and Central America, much of the agriculture is labor-intensive. About three to four percent of the population in Canada and the United States work at farming, while in Mexico, the farming population is about 28 percent.

Grains and livestock are raised on the plains of Canada and the United States. California, Florida, and Texas are notable producers of fruits and vegetables. Other agricultural products include cotton, dairy products, and sugar cane.

Forestry is a major industry in Canada and the western United States. Fishing is the most important industry in Greenland. Fishing is also done along the entire coast of the continent.

Canada, the United States, and Mexico consume enormous amounts of energy. A combination of nuclear, hydroelectric, coal, petroleum, and natural gas is necessary to supply the ever-increasing demand.

Major exports of the United States include food, chemicals, machinery, and transportation vehicles. Canada's major exports include chemicals, forest products, food, and metals. Mexico's major export is crude oil. Mexico and the Central American countries also export coffee and minerals.

The lumber industry thrives in the western United States and Canada.

Name: _____ Date: _____

Questions for Consideration

1. Proposals for drilling for oil in what region have brought protests?

   _____

2. What are North America's two most industrialized nations?

   _____

3. What percent of Mexico's population is engaged in agriculture?

   _____

4. In what two regions of North America is forestry a major industry?

   _____

5. In which North American country is fishing the major industry?

   _____

Matching

Place the letters for each region in front of the item in the list if that region is a major source of the item. More than one region may be a source for each item.

A. Canada   **B. Mexico**   **C. United States**   **D. Central America**

_____ 1. Coal   _____ 6. Iron ore

_____ 2. Coffee   _____ 7. Livestock

_____ 3. Forestry   _____ 8. Natural gas

_____ 4. Grains   _____ 9. Petroleum

_____ 5. Gold   _____ 10. Silver

DID YOU KNOW?

Corn was not known in Europe until Christopher Columbus brought some back from his first voyage to North America.

North America's Animal Life

North America has a large variety of animal species.

The natural habitats of most animals were decreased as humans settled in more of the continent, however. The loss of habitats, increased pollution, and the use of pesticides have continued to decrease the total number of animals living on the continent.

The passenger pigeon, Carolina parakeet, and heath hen all became extinct. The bison, whooping crane, bald eagle, and wild turkey came close to extinction. Through the efforts of conservationists, these species are slowly increasing in number.

In addition to domesticated animals, such as dogs, cats, horses, and livestock, many mammals live on the continent. Common North American mammals include the bat, beaver, coyote, fox, opossum, porcupine, raccoon, wolf, and a variety of rodents. The plains and prairies are home to antelope and deer, as well as burrowing animals, such as the gopher and the prairie dog.

Beaver, moose, and grizzly bears are some of the native animals of North America.

Larger mammals include bison, caribou, moose, deer, jaguar, oxen, puma, and sheep. The few remaining bison are usually raised in protected environments. Several varieties of bear also live in the northern regions. The world's largest bears include the grizzly bear and the polar bear.

North America is also home to a variety of reptiles. Poisonous snakes include the cottonmouth, rattlesnake, and copperhead. Other reptiles include a variety of nonpoisonous snakes, lizards (including chameleons), Gila monsters, and beaded lizards. The beaded lizard lives in Mexico and the southwestern United States; it is the world's only poisonous lizard.

North America's rivers and lakes are home to many species of freshwater fish. A variety of shellfish and finfish live in the coastal regions. Larger coastal inhabitants include whales, dolphins, and sharks.

The continent is also the habitat of over 800 species of birds. The variety of birds ranges from the tiny hummingbird to the large California condor. North America also provides a haven for a variety of marsh and inland water birds, including herons, ducks, pelicans, and geese. Birds of prey that live in North America include many species of eagles, hawks, and falcons. The Central America region is home to many colorful tropical varieties of birds.

Name: _____ Date: _____

Questions For Consideration

1. What three North American birds have become extinct?

   _____

   _____

2. Name two burrowing animals of the plains and prairies.

   _____

3. What are the world's largest bears?

   _____

4. What is the world's only poisonous lizard?

   _____

5. Name three North American birds of prey.

   _____

For Further Research

Choose one of the unusual animals mentioned in the narrative with which you are less familiar. Use at least two sources to help you. Write a paragraph in the space below describing this animal.

_____

_____

_____

_____

_____

_____

_____

_____

_____

_____

The Native People of North America

Mayan ruins of Mexico

When the first Europeans came to North America, many tribes of people, who later became known as Indians, lived throughout the continent.

Anthropologists believe that these people were descended from the people of northeast Asia. It is commonly believed that, approximately 20,000 to 30,000 years ago, hunters looking for new hunting grounds crossed a land bridge that connected Asia and North America. The land bridge, which no longer exists, was near what is now the Bering Strait. These early hunters continued to move south into the rest of North America and eventually into Central and South America.

The Native American tribes are divided into several major cultural groups. The native inhabitants of the northern arctic and subarctic regions are also known as **Northern Hunters**. They included the Aleuts, Chipewyan, and Inuit (known as Eskimo). They are hunters of caribou, polar bear, walrus, and whale.

The **Woodland group** inhabited the eastern part of the continent. They grew crops and used wood for housing, weapons, utensils, and canoes. Major woodland tribes included the Algonquian-speaking tribes of Delaware, Chippewa, Massachusett, Micmac, and Pequot. The Iroquois-speaking woodland tribes included the Cayuga, Mohawk, Oneida, Onondaga, and Seneca.

The **Plains tribes** lived in the west central region. They relied on hunting herds of bison, buffalo, deer, elk, and antelope. Plains tribes included the Arapaho, Blackfoot, Cheyenne, Comanche, Crow, Osage, Pawnee, Sioux, and Wichita.

Pueblo tribes lived in the southwestern United States and northern Mexico. They lived in houses made of **adobe**, which is a sun-dried clay brick. *Pueblo* is Spanish for "village." Pueblo tribes included the Apache, Hopi, Navajo, Yuma, and Zuni.

The **Pacific Northwest tribes** included the Chinook, Haida, Kwakiutl, Nootka, and Tlingit. The men were hunters and fishers, and the women gathered seeds, berries, and nuts for food.

The **California tribes** of Chumash, Karok, Maidu, Miwok, Pomo, and Yahi are also known as "seed gatherers of the desert." Their diets include berries, nuts, seeds, and roots. They are known for their basket weavers.

The **Great Basin and Plateau tribes** of the Flathead, Nez Percé, Paiute, Shoshone, Spokane, and Yakima lived in the west central region of what is now the United States and Canada.

The **Southeast tribes** of Alabama, Atakapa, Caddo, Catawba, Cherokee, Chickasaw, Choctaw, Natchez, Seminole, and Ticucua lived in what is now the southern and southeastern United States.

Mexican tribes included the Coahujltec, Concho, Lagunero, Seri, Yaqui, and the ancient Aztecs, Olmecs, and Toltecs. **Central America** is the home of the Mixtec, Tarascan, and Zapotec, as well as the ancient Mayan culture.

Totem pole of Northwest tribes

Name: _____ Date: _____

Questions for Consideration

1. From where did the first people of North America probably come?

   _____

2. How did the first people arrive in North America?

   _____

3. What is the common name for the Inuit tribe members?

   _____

4. What does *pueblo* mean in Spanish?

   _____

5. What are three of the ancient native cultures of Mexico?

   _____

Match the Cultures

Match the tribe in the left column with the culture listed in the right column.

_____ 1. Aleuts	A. California	
_____ 2. Apache	B. Central America	
_____ 3. Aztec	C. Great Basin & Plateau	
_____ 4. Cherokee	D. Mexico	
_____ 5. Chinook	E. Northern Hunters	
_____ 6. Comanche	F. Pacific Northwest	
_____ 7. Inuit	G. Plains	
_____ 8. Mayan	H. Pueblo	
_____ 9. Mohawk	I. Southeast	
_____ 10. Navajo	J. Woodland	
_____ 11. Nez Percé		
_____ 12. Seminole		
_____ 13. Sioux		
_____ 14. Spokane		
_____ 15. Yahi		

DID YOU KNOW?

Twenty-seven states of the United States have names derived from Native American languages.

The People of North America

Long before the arrival of European settlers, North America had a diverse group of indigenous people. An **indigenous** person is one who originally inhabited a certain location.

North America's indigenous people were referred to as "Indians" for many years. Today, the preferred term is "Native American." The term *Indian* has its origin from Christopher Columbus, who upon landing in the Americas thought he was in the East Indies islands.

The Europeans killed many of the native people in a series of conflicts. The Europeans also brought with them many diseases for which the native people had no defenses. Today's population of North America is mostly of European descent.

Over 35 percent of Canada's population is descended from the British Isles. About 25 percent is descended from the French. A large number of Canada's population are also of other European descent.

The United States' population is more diverse than Canada's. About 30 percent of America's people have a British or Irish heritage.

Clockwise from top left: The people of North America include those of Mestizo, Native American, European, Asian, and African descent.

Those of German and Scandinavian descent make up about 25 percent of the population. Blacks make up about 12 percent, Hispanics about nine percent, and those of Asian ancestry make up about three percent of the people of the United States.

Approximately 60 percent of the people of Mexico and Central America are mestizos. A *mestizo* is a person of mixed Native American and European (mostly Spanish) descent. It is estimated that about 30 percent of Mexican and Central American people are of pure Native American ancestry and about ten percent of pure European descent.

About 75 percent of North America's people live in urban areas. Three of the ten largest cities (Mexico City, New York City, and Los Angeles) are in North America. Mexico City is the world's second largest city. Only Tokyo, Japan, is larger.

English is the primary language in the United States and most of Canada. French is the main language of about one-third of Canadians. Spanish is the primary language of Mexico and Central America. Several Native American groups, including the Inuit (Eskimo), speak their native languages.

Christianity is the principal religion of North America. The great majority of Mexican and Central Americans, approximately 45 percent of Canadians, and 25 percent of U.S. inhabitants are Roman Catholic. Protestants make up about 50 percent of the population. The United States and Canada also have large communities of Jews and Eastern Orthodox Christians.

Name: _____ Date: _____

Questions for Consideration

1. What is an indigenous person?

   _____

2. Who first named Native Americans "Indians"?

   _____

3. What name is given to the descendants of Native Americans and the Spanish?

   _____

4. What is the world's second-largest city?

   _____

5. What is the major religion of North America?

   _____

What Percent?

Using information from the narrative page, fill in the blanks with the correct percentage of the population ancestry group for each nation.

The United States:

1. British and Irish _____

2. German and Scandinavian _____

3. Black _____

4. Hispanic _____

5. Asian _____

> **DID YOU KNOW?**
>
> Many historians believe that the first humans living in North America migrated from Asia over a prehistoric land connection near the present Bering Strait between Alaska and Russia.

Canada:

6. British _____

7. French _____

Mexico and Central America:

8. Mestizo _____

9. Native American _____

10. European _____

Canada

Both French and English explorers and settlers came to what is now known as Canada in the late seventeenth century. The British gained control when they captured the French city of Quebec in 1759.

In 1931, Canada was declared to be a self-governing dominion within the British Empire.

Today, it is a constitutional monarchy, with a parliamentary system of government. This means that the king or queen of England is the official head of state. However, elected members of Parliament run the country. A prime minister heads the government. The prime minister is the head of the political party that has the majority of members in the House of Commons, which is one of the two houses of Parliament.

Canada has ten provinces and three territories. The provinces are political divisions, much like states in the United States. The territories have more limited government, since so few people live there.

The eastern provinces include: Newfoundland, Nova Scotia, Prince Edward Island, and New Brunswick. Fishing is a major industry in these provinces. Other industries include mining, forestry, and tourism.

Quebec is Canada's largest province. Four out of five residents of Quebec speak French; French was declared the official language of Quebec in 1974. Many of Quebec's citizens want the province to separate from Canada and form its own country.

The central provinces are Ontario, Manitoba, Saskatchewan, and Alberta. Agriculture is a major industry in this region. Farmers raise cattle and a variety of crops. Industry and oil production have increased in the region in recent years.

British Columbia is Canada's most western province. The Rocky Mountains cover most of British Columbia's land. Vancouver, in British Columbia, is Canada's major port on the Pacific Ocean.

Canada's three territories are the Northwest Territories, the Yukon Territory, and Nunavut. These territories are mostly tundra, which has poor soil and a cold climate but is rich in mineral deposits. Nunavut separated from part of the Northwest Territories in 1999; it is the home to many of the Inuit, who are also known as Eskimos.

Canada and the United States share a 4,000-mile border. It is the world's longest unfortified border. The two nations are major trading partners. Trade with Canada is about 20 percent of the total of U.S. imports and exports. Canada's trade with the United States is about 70 percent of its total trade.

The Great Lakes and the St. Lawrence Seaway make up Canada's most important waterway. Completed in 1959, the Seaway allowed Montreal and Toronto to become ports for ocean-going vessels.

Niagara Falls is a spectacular waterfall located on the border between Canada and the United States.

Name: _____ Date: _____

Questions for Consideration

1. When did Canada become a self-governing dominion?

   _____

2. How many provinces does Canada have?

   _____

3. What is Canada's largest province?

   _____

4. What is Canada's newest territory?

   _____

5. When was the St. Lawrence Seaway completed?

   _____

Map Project

On the map below, label the following:

Alberta
British Columbia
Manitoba
New Brunswick
Newfoundland
Northwest Territories
Nova Scotia
Nunavut Territory
Ontario
Prince Edward Island
Quebec
Saskatchewan
Yukon Territory

The United States

The United States consists of fifty states. The first forty-eight states make up what is often referred to as the continental United States. Alaska and Hawaii are not connected by land to the other states.

Alaska contains much tundra and has a subarctic climate. The Hawaiian Islands are the tops of volcanoes in the Pacific Ocean and have a mild, almost tropical climate.

The continental states have three major regions. The eastern coastal area and the Appalachian Mountains were the earliest to be settled. The Great Plains stretch from the Appalachian Mountains in the east to the Rocky Mountains in the west. The Rocky Mountains, the Cascades Range, and the Sierra Nevadas divide the plains from the western coastal area.

The highest point in the United States is Mount McKinley in Alaska (20,320 feet; 6,194 m), and its lowest point is Death Valley in California (282 feet [86 m] below sea level). The highest point in the continental United States is Mount Whitney in California (14,494 feet [4,418 m] above sea level).

The Missouri, Mississippi, and Red Rock Rivers form the nation's major waterways and drain most of the central two-thirds of the land. The rivers have a combined length of 3,710 miles (5,971 km). The Mississippi is the longest river in the United States at 2,348 miles (3,778 km). The United States has many notable lakes, including the Great Lakes, as well as the Great Salt Lake in Utah.

The first European explorers included the Spanish under the leadership of Ponce de León and Hernando de Soto. They explored the southern and southeastern regions. Early French explorers included Jacques Cartier and Samuel de Champlain. Many early French settlers were fur trappers and traders. The first English settlement was in 1607. Eventually, the English gained control of most of the land, and the American colonies were ruled by England until the Revolutionary War.

From the time of its independence, the United States continued its westward expansion. It was rich in resources and soon became a leading manufacturing nation. The United States had not been very active in world events until after the Spanish-American War in the 1890s; however, after the war, America continued to grow as a major world power and industrial nation.

After World War II, the United States led world trade. As other nations recovered from the war and rebuilt their economies, they competed more with American trade. In the 1980s, United States imports from other countries exceeded its exports for the first time. Today, it continues to import more than it exports.

The population of the United States is over 270 million. Seventy-five percent of the population lives in urban areas. Two of the world's ten largest cities, New York City and Los Angeles, are in the United States.

River barges are a major mode of transportation for grains and raw materials in the country's interior.

Name: _____ Date: _____

Questions for Consideration

1. What is the highest point in the continental United States?

   _____

2. What is the longest river in the United States?

   _____

3. When did the United States' imports first exceed its exports?

   _____

4. What is the population of the United States?

   _____

5. Which two of the world's ten largest cities are in the United States?

   _____

Map Project

On the map below, label the following:

Appalachian
   Mountains
The Cascades
The Great Lakes
Great Salt Lake
Mississippi River
Missouri River
Rocky Mountains
The Sierra
   Nevadas

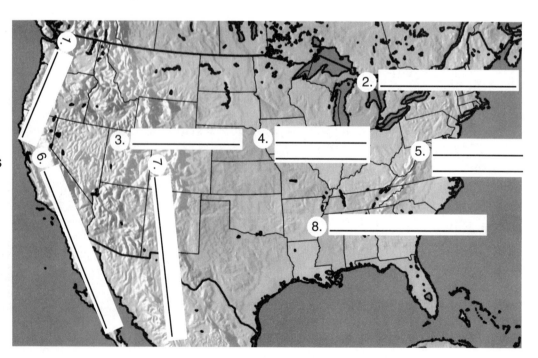

Mexico

The official name of Mexico is The United Mexican States. In Spanish, it is *Los Estados Unidos Mexicanos.*

Mexico shares a 1,933-mile (3,111-km) border with the United States. To the south, Mexico shares its border with Guatemala and Belize. Its western coast is on the Pacific Ocean, and the eastern coast is on the Gulf of Mexico.

Mexico is the largest Spanish-speaking country in the world. It is the second largest Roman Catholic nation in the world.

There is a colorful diversity in Mexico's culture. The major blend is of Spanish and Native American culture. Ancient civilizations included the Mayan, Olmec, Toltec, and Aztec Native American cultures. The Spanish conquest began in the sixteenth century and lasted for over 300 years. Mexico is a nation of contrast. It has ruins of ancient cities, churches from the Spanish colonial period, and modern skyscrapers.

Many mineral resources are found in Mexico, but there is limited farmland. Major crops include citrus fruits, beans, corn, bananas, pineapple, cotton, coffee, sugar cane, cacao, coca, wheat, oats, and rice.

Climate and geography vary in Mexico. It is a mountainous country with two mountain ranges enclosing a dry plateau. Mexico also contains large deserts, beautiful sand beaches, and jungle wetlands.

Mexico has one of the world's fastest-growing populations. Some of its people live in great wealth just a few miles from some of the world's largest slums. The unemployment rate continues to grow each year. The population of the Mexico City region is the largest urban area in the world. Mexico City itself (not including the adjoining area) is the world's second-largest city.

In addition to the problem of a fast-growing population, increasing pollution, crime, and drug usage and trafficking plague the country.

Mexico also has many popular tourist sites. In addition to the ancient Native American ruins, thousands of tourists visit Mexico's resort cities. Popular vacation resort destinations include Cancún, Acapulco, Mazatlán, Puerto Vallarta, and Veracruz.

Mexico is one of the fastest-growing industrial nations on earth. Major industries include petroleum and tourism. It may have the largest oil reserve in the Western Hemisphere. Auto plants and steel mills are increasing production each year.

Colorful *fiestas* or celebrations are part of Mexico's culture. Popular entertainment includes bullfights, soccer games, and rodeos. In addition to national holidays, Mexicans observe most Roman Catholic religious celebrations.

The Mexican culture has a great influence on the United States. Mexican art and music are increasing in popularity. Many Mexican foods such as tacos, burritos, and enchiladas are more popular than ever.

Mexico is famous for its colorful fiestas.

Name: _____ Date: _____

Questions for Consideration

1. What is Mexico's official name?

   _____

2. What is Mexico's official name in Spanish?

   _____

3. How long is the Mexican-United States border?

   _____

4. What is the largest urban area in the world?

   _____

5. What are Mexico's largest industries?

   _____

Map Project

On the map below, label the following:

Atlantic Ocean	Baja California
Gulf of California	Gulf of Mexico
Mexico City	Pacific Ocean
Yucatán Peninsula	

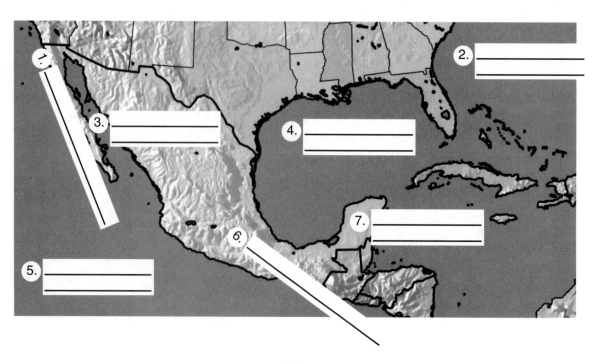

DID YOU KNOW?

September 15 is Mexico's Independence Day. It celebrates Mexico's 1810 rebellion against Spanish control.

Central America

Seven nations make up the region known as Central America.

Each of the Central American countries is unique. Most Guatemalans are descended from native tribes. Most Costa Ricans have European ancestors. Most people of El Salvador, Honduras, and Nicaragua are mestizo, or descendants of mixed native and Spanish backgrounds. Many citizens of Belize and Panama are of African descent.

Spanish is the major language of all of the Central American nations except Belize, which adopted English as its official language.

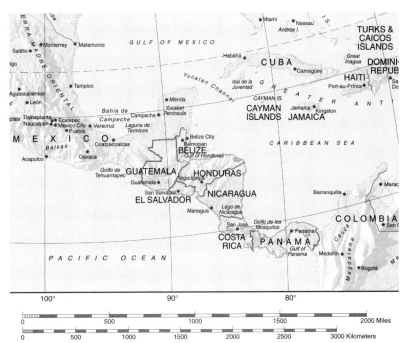

Agriculture is the major industry in the region. Bananas, coffee, cotton, rice, and sugar are all major exports. Ranchers raise sheep for wool and cattle for beef.

Fishing, mining, and forestry are other important industries. Pine, rosewood, and mahogany are harvested for exporting. Minerals found in the region include coal, copper, gold, iron ore, lead, nickel, and zinc. Fish and seafood caught for export include anchovies, lobster, shrimp, and tuna. The number of small factories has increased in the last several years, and tourism continues to grow in importance to Central America's economy.

Military governments and continued civil wars have long disrupted several Central American countries.

Guatemala was the site of the ancient Mayan civilization. In recent years, constant fighting has hurt its economy. Foreign investments and tourism have declined because of the political situation.

Belize was known as British Honduras until it gained its independence in 1981.

Honduras is Central America's poorest and least-developed nation. Unrest among its neighbors, Nicaragua, El Salvador, and Guatemala, constantly threatens Honduras' peace.

El Salvador is Central America's smallest and most densely-populated nation. For many years, only a few families owned the land. Unfortunately, the recent redistribution of the land has brought controversy and unrest in the nation.

Nicaragua recently suffered from fighting between the Sandinista and Contra soldiers. Today, it struggles with a population increase of 3.5 percent each year, making it difficult for the country to remain self-sufficient.

Costa Rica has the most stable government. It has been a peaceful republic since 1949. This has allowed it to have Central America's highest standard of living, literacy rate, and life expectancy.

Panama is famous for the canal that opened in 1914. The Panama Canal connects the Atlantic and Pacific Oceans, saving a long voyage around South America.

Name: _____   Date: _____

Questions for Consideration

1. Who were the ancestors of most Costa Ricans?

    _____

2. Which Central American country has English as its official language?

    _____

3. Which is Central America's poorest nation?

    _____

4. Which Central American country has the most stable government?

    _____

5. When was the Panama Canal opened?

    _____

> **DID YOU KNOW?**
>
> Chicle, a sap from the sapodilla tree grown in Guatemala and Belize, is used to make chewing gum.

Map Project

On the map below, label the following:

Belize   Caribbean Sea   Costa Rica   El Salvador
Guatemala   Gulf of Mexico   Honduras   Nicaragua
Pacific Ocean   Panama

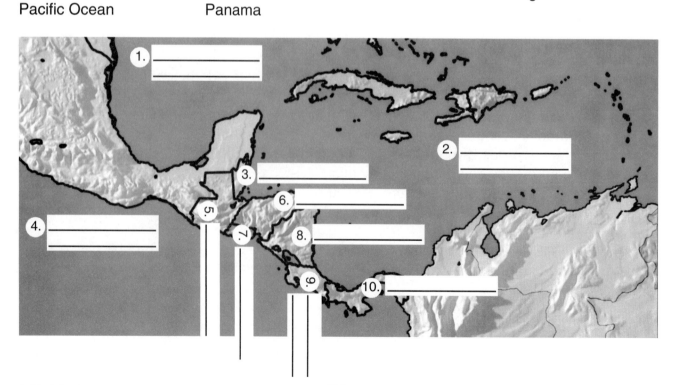

North America's Islands

The continent of North America has hundreds of islands off its coasts. Most of the islands, such as Canada's Prince Edward Island and Vancouver Island, and the United States' islands of Manhattan and the Florida Keys, are part of each nearby country. Other islands, such as Greenland and the Caribbean Islands, are independent nations.

Greenland is the world's largest island. Located in the North Atlantic Ocean, it is about  one-third the size of the continental United States. It is a self-governing part of Denmark. Sheet glaciers, called **ice caps**, cover over 80 percent of Greenland. The island's population is about 50,000, which includes a large Eskimo population.

The Caribbean Islands are also referred to as the West Indies. They include the Bahamas, the Greater Antilles, and the Lesser Antilles.

The Bahamas are a group of over 700 islands. Only 22 of these islands are inhabited. Even though they are in the Atlantic Ocean, they are often referred to as Caribbean islands.  The Bahamas are an independent member of the British Commonwealth.

The capital of the Bahamas, Nassau, is a popular tourist destination. Tourism is the major industry. Over two-thirds of the population is involved in the tourist industry. Christopher Columbus probably landed on one of the Bahamas, San Salvador, in 1492.

The **Greater Antilles** include the islands of Cuba, Hispaniola (Haiti and the Dominican Republic), Jamaica, and Puerto Rico.

The **Lesser Antilles** include the Virgin Islands. Other Lesser Antilles such as Trinidad, Tobago, and Barbados are considered by most geographers to be part of South America.

Cuba is the largest and most populous of all of the West Indies. Havana, its capital, is only 92 nautical miles (170 km) from Florida. Chris-  topher Columbus visited in 1492, and the Spanish began controlling the island in 1511. Cuba remained under Spanish control until the Spanish-American War in 1898. It then came under U.S. protection. In 1958, a revolution put a communist government into power under the leadership of Fidel Castro.

Agriculture is Cuba's major industry. Important crops include sugar cane and tobacco. Tourism is also a major industry.

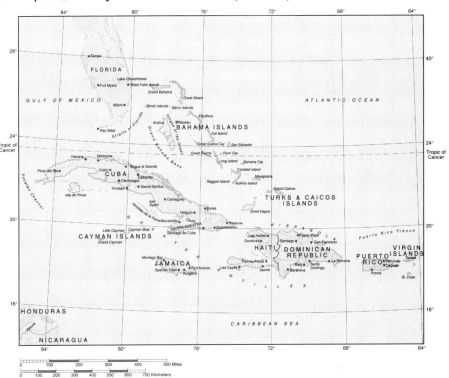

Puerto Rico is another popular tourist destination. Agriculture was the major industry until the mid-1950s when factories became more plentiful. Major crops include sugar cane,  tobacco, and coffee. In 1952, Puerto Rico became a commonwealth with an association with the United States.

Puerto Ricans are United States citizens. Occasionally, groups of citizens promote Puerto Rico to become the fifty-first state of the United States.

The Dominican Republic and Haiti share an island named **Hispaniola**; however, the two countries have little in common. Christopher Columbus landed on this island in 1492.

The Dominican Republic has a Hispanic culture, and most of its population is White or mulatto. Its capital, Santo Domingo, is the oldest city in the western hemisphere. Spanish settlers arrived there in 1496.

 **Haiti** has a strong French influence in its culture. Most of its people are of African and French descent. Haiti is a poor, overpopulated country.

In recent years, both The Dominican Republic and Haiti have had much political strife. This has harmed tourism and other economic development.

Jamaica is a mountainous island. Christopher Columbus visited the island during his 1494 voyage. It came under Spanish rule until the British took control in 1655. It then became an independent part of the British Commonwealth in 1962.

For many years, plantation owners brought over African slaves to work in the sugar cane and coffee fields. Agriculture is still an important part of Jamaica's economy, but today, the island's major industry is tourism.

The Virgin Islands are divided into the British Virgin Islands and the United States Virgin Islands. The British Virgin Islands include 36 islands. They have a total land area of 59  square miles (153 sq. km). The United States Virgin Islands include fifty islands. They have 136 square miles (352 sq. km). St. Croix, St. Thomas, and St. John are three of the largest islands. The United States purchased the American Virgin Islands from Denmark in 1917.

The islands have a mild climate and beautiful scenery. Tourism is the major industry in the islands. Many of the islands' people make craft items to sell to the tourists. Because there is duty-free and sales-tax-free shopping, tourists buy imported goods from around the world in Virgin Island cities. Electronics, jewelry, liquor, tobacco, and textile products are some of the major items sold in the U.S. Virgin Islands.

Name: _____ Date: _____

Questions for Consideration

1. What is the world's largest island?

    _____

2. How many islands are in the Bahamas?

    _____

3. What is the capital of Cuba?

    _____

4. Puerto Ricans are citizens of what country?

    _____

5. What is Jamaica's largest industry?

    _____

Map Project

On the map below, label the following:

Atlantic Ocean
Bahamas
Caribbean Sea
Cuba
Dominican Republic
Gulf of Mexico
Haiti
Jamaica
Puerto Rico
Virgin Islands

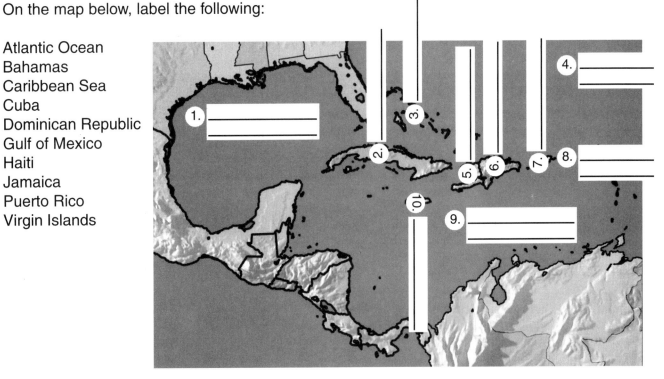

Answer Keys

THE CONTINENTS (page 3)
1. A large landmass completely or mostly surrounded by water
2. Just over 29 percent
3. Continental drift
4. Plate tectonics
5. Volcanoes and earthquakes

MAP PROJECT (page 3)
Teacher check map. Use the map on page 1 as a guide.

THE CONTINENT OF NORTH AMERICA (page 6)
1. The land of the Western Hemisphere
2. Death Valley, California
3. Mount McKinley, Alaska
4. Mackenzie River
5. Erie, Huron, Michigan, Ontario, Superior

MAP PROJECT (page 6)
Teacher check map. Use the map on page 5 as a guide.

NORTH AMERICA'S CLIMATE (page 8)
1. Arctic, tropical
2. Cold winters and hot summers; adequate precipitation
3. Humid subtropical
4. Marine west coast and Mediterranean
5. Central American countries

CLIMATE ZONES (page 8)
(Answers may vary.)
1. Arctic: bitterly cold, long nights; short days
2. Humid continental: cold winters; hot summers; adequate precipitation
3. Humid subtropical: warm winters; hot, humid summers
4. Highland: mild winters; warm summers; significant rainfall
5. Desert: hot days; cool nights; very little rainfall

6. Tropical: hot temperatures and much rainfall throughout the year

NORTH AMERICA'S RESOURCES AND INDUSTRIES (page 10)
1. Alaska
2. Canada and the United States
3. 28 percent
4. Canada, western United States
5. Greenland

MATCHING (page 10)
1. A, C
2. B, D
3. A, C
4. A, C
5. A, B, C, D
6. A, B, C
7. A, C
8. A, B, C
9. A, B, C
10. A, B, C, D

NORTH AMERICA'S ANIMAL LIFE (page 12)
1. Passenger pigeon, Carolina parakeet, heath hen
2. Gopher, prairie dog
3. Polar, grizzly
4. Beaded lizard
5. Eagle, hawk, falcon

THE NATIVE PEOPLE OF NORTH AMERICA (page 14)
1. Asia
2. By crossing a land bridge
3. Eskimo
4. Village
5. Aztec, Olmec, Toltec

MATCH THE CULTURES (page 14)
1. E
2. H
3. D
4. I
5. F
6. G
7. E
8. B
9. J
10. H
11. C
12. I
13. G
14. C
15. A

PEOPLE OF NORTH AMERICA (page 16)
1. Someone who originally inhabited a location
2. Christopher Columbus
3. Mestizos
4. Mexico City
5. Christianity

WHAT PERCENT? (page 16)
1. 30%
2. 25%
3. 12%
4. 9%
5. 3%
6. 35%
7. 25%
8. 60%
9. 30%
10. 10%

CANADA (page 18)
1. 1931
2. Ten
3. Quebec
4. Nunavut
5. 1959

MAP PROJECT (page 18)
1. Yukon Territory
2. Northwest Territories
3. Nunavut Territory
4. British Columbia
5. Alberta
6. Saskatchewan
7. Manitoba
8. Ontario
9. Quebec
10. Newfoundland
11. Prince Edward Island
12. New Brunswick
13. Nova Scotia

THE UNITED STATES (page 20)
1. Mount Whitney
2. Mississippi River
3. In the 1980s
4. Over 270 million
5. New York City and Los Angeles

MAP PROJECT (page 20)
1. The Cascades
2. Great Lakes
3. Great Salt Lake
4. Missouri River
5. Appalachian Mts.
6. Sierra Nevada
7. Rocky Mountains
8. Mississippi River

MEXICO (page 22)
1. The United Mexican States
2. Los Estados Unidos Mexicanos
3. 1,933 miles (3,111 km)
4. The Mexico City area
5. Petroleum and tourism

MAP PROJECT (page 22)
1. Baja California
2. Atlantic Ocean
3. Gulf of California
4. Gulf of Mexico
5. Pacific Ocean
6. Mexico City
7. Yucatán Peninsula

CENTRAL AMERICA (page 24)
1. Europeans
2. Belize
3. Honduras
4. Costa Rica
5. 1914

MAP PROJECT (page 24)
1. Gulf of Mexico
2. Caribbean Sea
3. Belize
4. Pacific Ocean
5. Guatemala
6. Honduras
7. El Salvador
8. Nicaragua
9. Costa Rica
10. Panama

NORTH AMERICA'S ISLANDS (page 27)
1. Greenland
2. Over 700
3. Havana
4. The United States
5. Tourism

MAP PROJECT (page 27)
1. Gulf of Mexico
2. Cuba
3. Bahamas
4. Atlantic Ocean
5. Haiti
6. Dominican Rep.
7. Puerto Rico
8. Virgin Islands
9. Caribbean Sea
10. Jamaica

Bibliography

Individual books:

Bock, Judy. *Scholastic Encyclopedia of the United States.* Scholastic Reference, 1997.

Cooper, Michael. *Klondike Fever—The Famous Gold Rush of 1898.* Clarion Books, 1989.

Curlee, Lynn. *Into the Ice, The Story of Arctic Exploration.* Houghton Mifflin, 1997.

Kingfisher Young People's Encyclopedia of the United States. Kingfisher, 1994.

Kramme, Michael. *Mexico.* Mark Twain Media/Carson-Dellosa Publishing Company, Inc., 1999.

Malcolm, Andrew H. *The Land and People of Canada.* Harper Collins Pubs., 1991.

St. George, Judith. *Panama Canal: Gateway to the World.* Putnam, 1989.

Series:

Cultures of the World (Series published by Benchmark Books). Each book was published between 1994 and 2001, contains 128 pages. Countries included: *Bahamas, Belize, Canada, Costa Rica, Cuba, Dominican Republic, El Salvador, Guatemala, Haiti, Honduras, Jamaica, Panama, Puerto Rico*, and *Nicaragua*

Major World Nations (Series published by Chelsea House). Each book was published between 1997 and 2001, contains 32 to 94 pages. Countries included: *Bahamas, Canada, Cuba, Dominican Republic, El Salvador, Guatemala, Haiti, Honduras, Jamaica, Nicaragua, Panama*, and *Puerto Rico*

Enchantment of the World (Series published by Children's Press). Each book was published between 1999 and 2002, contains 44–48 pages. Countries included: *Bahamas, Canada, Costa Rica, Cuba, Dominican Republic, El Salvador, Greenland, Honduras, Mexico*, and *Panama*